P9-DXF-893

A Hot Issue

Kathleen Winkler

Enslow Publishers, Inc.

40 Industrial Road   PO Box 38
Box 398   Aldershot
Berkeley Heights, NJ 07922   Hants GU12 6BP
USA   UK

http://www.enslow.com

Library of Congress Cataloging-in-Publication Data

Winkler, Kathleen
    Date rape : a hot issue / Kathleen Winkler.
       p. cm. — (Hot issues)
    Includes bibliographical references and index.
    Summary: Discusses the myths and facts surrounding acquaintance, or date, rape, of both men and women, the physical and psychological consequences, ways to stay safe, and what to do if sexually assaulted.
    ISBN 0-7660-1198-4
    1. Acquaintance rape—United States—Juvenile literature.
2. Dating violence—United States—Juvenile literature. 3. Rape—United States—Prevention—Juvenile literature. [1. Acquaintance rape. 2. Dating violence. 3. Rape.] I. Title. II. Series.
HV6561.W56   1999
362.883—dc21   98-41352
                                         CIP
                                         AC

Printed in the United States of America

10 9 8 7 6 5 4 3 2 1

To Our Readers:
All Internet addresses in this book were active and appropriate when we went to press. Any comments or suggestions can be sent by e-mail to Comments@enslow.com or to the address on the back cover.

Illustration Credits:
AP/Wide World Photos, p. 29; AP/Wide World Photos, Richard Freeda, p. 12; © Corel Corporation, pp. 1, 4, 11, 20; Skjold Photographs, pp. 16, 28, 41, 47, 50.

Cover Illustration: © Corel Corporation

Contents

*B*oth girls and guys need to decide how physically intimate they want to be with another person before they even go out on a date.

Chapter 1

He Was My Friend— How Could He Do This?

Heather's Story

Heather was only fourteen when she first met Kevin. He was a year older and seemed so mature, so exciting, so out of reach. She never thought he'd actually be interested in her. But they started hanging out with the same crowd. Soon it seemed that Kevin actually liked her. He'd sit next to her at the games or at the pizza place. She'd catch him looking at her. Just after she turned sixteen, Kevin asked her out. It didn't take Heather long to say yes. "I thought he was going to be my answer to everything," she says. "Finally someone was attracted to me, liked me, accepted me just as I was."[1]

After six months of dating, Kevin started pressuring Heather to have sex. She really didn't want to, but most of her girlfriends were sexually active and they warned Heather she'd lose Kevin if she said no. Heather didn't have a close relationship with her mother, so she didn't feel comfortable asking her about it. Not wanting to lose her first real boyfriend, she finally said yes. They had intercourse a couple of times, but Heather never really felt quite right about it.

"By the end of the summer I started making up excuses not to see him," she remembers. "I really wanted to break up, but I didn't have the nerve to do it. Part of it was that we had had sex. I felt guilty for having given in and now saying 'This isn't going to last forever after all.'"[2]

Just before school started, Heather decided she had to break up. Kevin was spending the last week of the summer at his grandparents' house. Heather drove out there to talk to him. His grandparents were gone for the day.

"We were in his bedroom talking," Heather recalls. "I was telling him that this relationship was just not going to work. He got angry, saying, 'Why, why? We can make it work.' He pulled me down on the bed next to him and started kissing me."[3]

Heather kept protesting, "No, back off!" but Kevin kept kissing her, more and more forcefully. Then he started pulling off her blouse and jeans.

"At that point I started to black out and become numb, so I don't remember all of what happened," she says.

> I remember saying no over and over, and him saying, 'You know you want it, why are you pushing me away?' I remember him getting on top of me and just doing it while I was lying there trying to make my body numb, trying not to feel it. When he was finished I got up and left and I never saw him again.[4]

At the time Heather didn't think of it as rape.

"I thought I had done something wrong and he was punishing me, especially since he was my boyfriend and we had had sex before. I thought maybe I hadn't said no clearly enough."[5]

Heather carried the secret of what Kevin did to her around inside for many years. She didn't tell anyone. "I had constant questions in my head, though," she says. "What did I do wrong? How could I have prevented it?"[6]

It wasn't until six years later that she started to think, "Wait a minute, that was rape!" She read a couple of books about date rape and became even more convinced.

After she graduated from high school, Heather developed an eating disorder. She feels now that she was covering up several issues—low self-esteem and a family that didn't get along very well, as well as the rape. When she went into therapy, she told her counselor about the rape. The counselor helped her see that even though Kevin hadn't used a weapon beyond his bigger size and hadn't slapped or beat her, it was still rape. That even though she had had sex with him before, it was still rape. "I didn't come out of it all black and blue, it didn't happen in some dark alley, it was in the middle of the afternoon on a bright sunny day, in his grandparents' guest room—but it was rape," she says now.[7]

Because she had said NO.

It took Heather a long time to start dating again, even longer to realize that sex can be warm, loving, and gentle. Even now, married to a kind, caring man, she still has moments when her mind flashes back to the rape. At one time she thought about reporting it, but she doesn't know where Kevin is now, and she decided that after seven years she didn't want to revisit that time in her life. "But I've reached the point where I can look at what he did and say, 'That was wrong; it was rape,'" she says. "It took me a long time to accept the fact that it doesn't matter if it's someone you know, it doesn't matter if you've had sex before—if you say no, then no means no. If he doesn't stop, then you've been violated."[8]

Jenny's Story

It was different for Jenny. She wasn't dating the boy who raped her. She didn't even know him very well. He was the son of one of her favorite teachers. She knew his mom and dad, and their two families had done a few things together.

Jenny was very young, just a few months past her thirteenth birthday. It was a Saturday morning. She and her friend, Nicole, were going shopping together. Jenny got to Nicole's house a little early. Nicole had gone to the library, her mom said, and would be back soon. Nicole's mom and dad were leaving to do their own errands, but they said Jenny was welcome to wait. Jenny had been in their house many times before, so she felt perfectly comfortable being alone there.

A few minutes after Nicole's parents left, the doorbell rang. Three older guys, seventeen or so, stood on the porch. They had come to pick up Nicole's older sister, but she wasn't home, either. Jenny knew the three guys, especially the youngest one, her teacher's son. She invited them in to wait.

At first, sitting around with the older guys was kind of fun. They were talking to her, making her feel like a friend, even though she was so much younger. She thought they might have been drinking before they came, but the attention was flattering. Jenny went into the kitchen to get them sodas, but

What a Victim May Feel After a Date Rape

✓ sadness
✓ shock
✓ horror
✓ disbelief that this could happen
✓ anger
✓ fear that it will happen again
✓ fear of what others will think
✓ shame, embarrassment
✓ guilt, self-blame
✓ relief at having survived
✓ desire to put it all behind, not to think about it
✓ fear of seeing the rapist again at school, work, or in the neighborhood

What the Victim's Friends and Family May Feel After a Date Rape

✓ emotional pain
✓ anger at the rapist
✓ fear that it could happen to them also
✓ fear that they will say the wrong thing
✓ guilt because they weren't able to protect the victim
✓ at a loss about how to help
✓ anger at the victim for "taking a chance," doing something "dumb," or breaking a rule
✓ desire to forget it happened, not deal with it
✓ relief that the victim survived
✓ desire to protect the victim so that it can't happen again

two of the guys decided to go on ahead and leave the teacher's son to wait for Nicole's sister. "That's when it happened," she says. "He had a knife. The next thing I knew I was on the kitchen floor and he was raping me." She pauses and quietly adds, "It wasn't a real pleasant thing."[9]

Like Heather, Jenny didn't tell anyone what had happened to her. She wasn't confused about whether or not it was rape—there was no doubt in her mind. But she was too scared to say anything. "I had so much respect for the guy's father," she says. "I didn't want to put his family through anything, or mine. I knew it would tear both families apart if I told."[10]

A few weeks later the guy called Nicole's older sister when Jenny was at their house. He asked to talk to Jenny. When she heard the familiar voice, Jenny hung up on him. "I couldn't believe he had the nerve to try to have a conversation with me!" she says.[11] "I don't think I dealt with the whole thing very well at first," Jenny continues, looking back ten years later.

> I think I just kind of blocked it out, pushed it back. For a long time it wasn't really a problem because I was so young and I didn't date. But later, when I started going on dates, I got very nervous. It started resurfacing. I'd be on a date and be afraid it would progress to that again.[12]

Thinking back, Jenny says she would change several things if she were in the same situation. First, she wouldn't let anybody into an empty house with her even if she knew the person. "But I just didn't suspect that they would do anything," she says.[13]

She also would avoid spending time with guys who were a lot older. "I don't think somebody who is thirteen has much in common with someone who is seventeen," she says. "I'd be suspicious of a much older guy/younger girl relationship."[14] While younger girls may be flattered by attention from older guys and think they are mature enough to handle it, too often they aren't, she reflects.

Drinking is a red flag, she says. "If a guy has been drinking, it would be good to be more cautious, because sometimes people who are drinking aren't themselves."[15]

*M*any times, beer and other alcoholic beverages can negatively affect a person's actions.

Jenny now regrets not telling anyone, even though she feels that eventually she worked it through successfully on her own just by thinking about it. "But I wouldn't try to deal with it on my own again," she says. "It isn't easy. It would have helped to talk to someone."[16]

Jenny also wishes she'd charged the young man.

It's too late now for me; I don't know where he is anymore. But I'd advise anyone it happens to to do something. Hard as it might be to go through with, it's better. If you charge the person, at least you'd have the satisfaction of knowing that he didn't get away with it.[17]

*A*lex Kelly is shown being taken to court by sheriff's deputies to stand trial for raping a high school girl. He was later convicted and sentenced to sixteen years in prison.

These two young women had experiences that were the same in some ways and different in others. Although they were both raped, one was attacked by a boy she was dating (date rape) and the other by someone she knew but had no relationship with (acquaintance rape).

Although you might think from their stories that rapists always get away with it because both of theirs did, that's not always true. In one highly publicized case, an eighteen-year-old wrestling star, named Alex Kelly was accused of offering a high school girl a ride home from a party, and then raping her in the backseat of a Jeep Wagoneer. On the eve of his trial, Kelly fled to Europe, where he spent eight years traveling and avoiding the FBI. When he returned to the United States, he was immediately tried for the rape, convicted, and sentenced to sixteen years in prison.[18]

Chapter 2

It Isn't Always the Stranger Lurking in the Bushes

When you hear the word *rape*, what do you think of? A man hiding in the bushes who grabs a woman as she walks by? A man in a ski mask climbing through a woman's bedroom window? Do you ever think of it as rape when a boy and girl are on a date, he wants sex and she doesn't, so he just sort of pushes her a little to get her to cooperate?

Our society is confused about what rape is. Many people think that if it isn't a stranger jumping out of the bushes or climbing through a window, it does not qualify as rape.

That's not what the law says.

Defining Rape

"In the old days there was no question about what rape was," says Janine Arseneau, a social worker at a rape crisis center. "It was intercourse, it involved penetrating another person's body—that's the image most people have when they talk about rape. But it's actually much broader than that."[1]

According to the law, says Amy Judy, a lawyer with the Wisconsin Coalition Against Sexual Assault, sexual assault is sexual contact that is forced or done without the person's consent. Rape is a form of sexual assault that includes sexual intercourse.[2]

Different states use different terms for the types of sexual assault. Some divide it into first-, second-, third-, or fourth-degree sexual assault. Others states use different terms.

Twenty-eight states define rape as sex without consent—if the victim doesn't give permission or stays quiet, it's rape. In the other states, rape is an act of force—the victim has to show the rapist that the action is unwanted (keeping quiet would mean consent in those states). Some states include oral or anal sex as rape; some define it only as vaginal sex. In many states, a person under a certain age is not considered able to give consent, so sexual contact with a person under that age is always rape. In many

Who Rapes?

Percentages of types of perpetrators in adult rape cases

✓Friends........................20%

✓Husbands 16%

✓Boyfriends 14%

✓Neighbors, coworkers.........9%

✓Other........................41%

Source: National Women's Study, as reported in "How to Spot and Resist the Rapist You Know" by Susan Jacoby in *Glamour*, February 1994.

states, as well as under federal law, having sexual contact with someone who is unconscious or under the influence of drugs or alcohol is also rape because that person can't give consent. If you want to know what the law in your state is, call a rape crisis line, a group for sexual assault prevention, or your state attorney general's office.

What, Then, Is Date Rape?

"Date or acquaintance rape is not a legal term," says Amy Judy. "In the legal system you won't find a special definition of date rape—it's all covered under the rape laws."[3]

Date or acquaintance rape is a subcategory of rape. It means sex without consent between two people who know each other, whether they are dating (as Heather was) or are just acquainted (as in Jenny's story). "The law shouldn't care if the perpetrator and victim knew each other," says Amy Judy. "What's important is whether or not the victim gave consent."[4]

A woman's risk of being assaulted by someone she knows is much greater than her risk of being raped by a stranger—78 percent of all sexual assaults are committed by someone the victim knows.[5] Women from ages eighteen to twenty-nine run the greatest risk,[6] although recent studies show that even junior-high-school girls are at risk. One in four college women were the victims of rape or attempted rape, according to a survey done at Kent State University, and 84 percent of them knew the rapist. Of these rapes, 57 percent were committed while the rapist and victim were on a date.[7]

Just to make things simpler, in this book we will

*U*niversities are not always safe havens for young women. A recent survey found that 25 percent of college women have been the victims of rape or attempted rape.

use the term *date rape*; the term will also cover rape by friends and acquaintances.

Myths About Date Rape

Remember that stranger in the bushes or climbing though the window? Those kinds of rapes certainly happen—far too often. But some people have the idea that they are the only kind of rape.

That's a myth.

People believe a lot of other myths about rape, too, say Janine Arseneau, Amy Judy, and Robin Warshaw (author of *I Never Called It Rape*). Some of those mistaken ideas are very common.

Many people think the greatest danger of rape comes from a stranger, but the fact is, a woman is much more likely to be raped by someone she knows. Many women think that the person who would rape her will look like a rapist—dirty, ugly, like a criminal. But he's much more likely to resemble the guy who sits next to you in class, works with you, or lives next door.

Women sometimes take on a terrible burden of guilt, thinking that they asked to be raped if they had too much to drink, went to the guy's room to listen to music or talk, or got in his car. But the fact is that doing those things is never asking to be raped. Doing them doesn't mean a woman is consenting to have sex with a man.

Other women feel guilty because they think they didn't fight back hard enough, but the fact is that rape is rape whether or not the victim fought. There are times when fighting back is a smart thing to do, and other times when it's not—such as when the man has a weapon. Women also sometimes feel that if the guy didn't use a weapon, it wasn't rape.

Myths and Facts About Rape

Myth	Rape is committed by strangers.
Fact	You are more likely to be raped by someone you know.
Myth	Men who rape women look wild, ugly, violent.
Fact	Most rapists look like "the guy next door."
Myth	You asked for it by drinking, going to a guy's room, or getting in his car.
Fact	Drinking, going to a guy's room, or getting in his car doesn't mean you are saying, "yes," to sex.
Myth	If you didn't fight back, you weren't raped.
Fact	If someone has sex with you against your will, you have been raped, fight or not.
Myth	If he didn't use a weapon, you weren't raped.
Fact	It doesn't matter—gun, knife, alcohol, a drug, his larger body—if you didn't want it, it's rape.
Myth	If you've had sex before, it's not rape.
Fact	Whether you were a virgin or sexually experienced, whether you had sex with the rapist before doesn't matter—if you didn't want it, it's rape.
Myth	If the guy has spent money, it's not rape because you owe him sex.
Fact	Sex is never owed to anyone; it is never a payment.
Myth	Kissing or sexual touching before means it isn't rape.
Fact	Agreeing to some sexual things doesn't mean agreeing to intercourse. You can say no at any time even if he is already turned on.
Myth	A turned-on guy has to have sex, or he will be in pain.
Fact	There is no biological proof that a guy will be in pain if he doesn't have sex once he's turned on.
Myth	I must make my date happy; if he wants sex, I owe him.
Fact	More nonsense. Your self-respect is far more important than pleasing your date.
Myth	No doesn't really mean "no," it means "try harder."
Fact	No does mean no. It doesn't mean "try harder" or "try in a different way."
Myth	He, I, or we were drunk, so it wasn't rape.
Fact	Either party's being drunk never excuses rape.

But sex against a woman's will is always rape whether the man uses a gun, a knife, or just his bigger, stronger body to force it.

If you've had sex before, does that mean you can't be raped? Of course not. It doesn't matter if you've never had sex before or if you've had it with many men or even if you've had it with that particular guy before. If you don't want it, it's rape.

Some young women think that if the guy paid for her movie ticket, pizza, or prom flowers, then she owes him sex. But it doesn't matter how much money he's spent—a woman never owes a man sex even if he spent a fortune on her!

How about if you were kissing him or letting him touch you in a sexual way? Is it still rape? The answer is yes. Just because you've agreed to do some sexual things doesn't mean you've agreed to have intercourse. You have the right to say "no" at any time, at any stage of kissing or touching, and to have that "no" respected. Even if he is very turned on, you have the right to say stop. He doesn't have the right to keep going. And don't believe the myth that when a guy gets turned on, he has to have sex, or he will be in pain. If a guy is uncomfortable, it's because he's not getting what he wants, not because he is experiencing physical pain.

A lot of women think that because an attractive guy has asked them out, they have to be sure to keep him happy on their date. If that means having sex, they'd better go along, or he won't have fun. Of course you care if your date is having fun, but your values and self-respect are far more important than pleasing your date. You have to do what will make you feel good about yourself.

Some guys believe that no doesn't really mean

*M*any young people mistakenly believe that a girl owes a guy sex if he spends money on her on a date.

no, it just means "try harder." "Oh, sure, that's what girls have to tell us," they may think. But the fact is that no does mean no. It doesn't mean "try harder" or "try in a different way."

What about losing your self-control because you've been drinking? "He was drunk, I was drunk, we were both drunk, so it wasn't rape," you might think. The fact that either person is drunk never excuses rape.[8]

Guys Can Be Raped, Too

It is most often women who are raped. But guys can be raped, too. Some experts estimate that about 10 percent of victims seeking help at rape crisis centers are male.[9]

In most cases men are raped by other men, but

there are a few cases in which women have raped men. How can a guy be raped by a woman? It is possible to stimulate a man into having an erection even if he doesn't want one. Cases of female-male rape often involve child abuse.

Men raping other men is more common. Again, it is often but not always an older man taking advantage of a younger boy. Sometimes, when the boy is much younger, it's called child sexual abuse. That's also rape.

The emotional result for a man is just as devastating as for a woman.[10] Besides the other emotional effects, a young man may wonder if being raped makes him a homosexual. It doesn't.

Chapter 3

Who Does This and Why?

It's a myth that a man who rapes is always a violent, wild-eyed stranger who is mentally ill. The truth is, he's probably not any of those things. Yes, some rapists are sick people. Some are men who hate women and use rape to express their hostility, to frighten and punish their victims. But many date rapists are otherwise nice guys who don't look like "the type" to rape.

Men Who Rape Dates

A lot of guys who have committed date rape don't even realize they have done so. They just think they got a little physical to "encourage" the girl to have sex. Often they think the girl really wanted it and was just saying no so that she could feel like a "nice" girl.

How could any guy pick up such a wrong impression?

Part of it is the society girls and guys grow up in. "We've been murky in our definitions about what is rape," says Janine Arseneau, a rape crisis counselor.

"Kids aren't always taught very clearly that a woman has the right to say no."[1]

Too often, she says, girls grow up being taught that their "job" in life is to look pretty, smile, and make everyone happy. Girls who grow up with that attitude may not realize they have the right to decide if and when they want to have sex, and to say no if they don't.

Some boys, on the other hand, grow up learning that a real man is aggressive, that he gets what he wants, and that when he "scores" (has sex with a girl), it's a victory.

Those beliefs are stereotypes. Most stereotypes are destructive because they put people into categories—all girls, all boys, all blacks, all whites—and everyone in the category is viewed the same way. People are individuals, and all are different. People who believe stereotypes can easily fall into the trap of not thinking of another person as a real human being. So guys who think that girls are there to make them happy and owe them sex can commit

Relationships Between Rapists and Victims

✓ Well known to the victim 35%

✓ Casual acquaintances 21%

✓ Relatives............................. 11%

✓ Strangers 33%

Source: 1994 Bureau of Census data, reported in "Most Recent U.S. Rape and Sexual Assault Statistics," <www.kidpower.org/state/stats1.html>.

date rape and not really know it. But the law doesn't care what stereotype you believed in. It only cares whether or not the victim gave consent.

Another destructive message some children learn at home and from television, according to Arseneau, is that if you ask Mom long enough for a cookie, she'll get tired of saying no and finally give in. Some guys think that applies to sex, too. They think that if a guy just keeps asking a girl, he can wear down her resistance, and she'll finally say yes. That persistent pressure is a form of date rape, too.

Here are some other reasons that a guy might rape someone he knows or is dating:

> He wants to control, punish, or humiliate the victim.

> He thinks he is entitled to sex whenever he wants it.

> He just thinks he can get away with it.[2]

> He thinks because a girl is wearing sexy clothes, that means she wants to have sex.

One study of nearly four hundred high school guys and girls found that if a girl was wearing something revealing when she was date raped, there was a much greater chance that she would be blamed.[3] The truth is, it is never the victim's fault, no matter what she was wearing.

A nice guy turning into a date rapist is more common than we'd like to think. When *Ms.* magazine did an anonymous survey of college students' attitudes toward rape, they were surprised to find that out of 2,971 college men, 187 admitted raping a woman, 157 more said they had attempted rape, 327 said they had tried to pressure a woman to have sex with them, and 854 said they had touched

What Rights Do I Have in a Relationship

✓ I have the right to an equal relationship.

✓ I have the right not to be dominated.

✓ I have the right to act one way with one person and a different way with someone else.

✓ I have the right to change my mind whenever I want to.

✓ I have the right to reject unwanted attention.

✓ I have the right to start a relationship slowly.

✓ I have the right to say, "I want to know you better before I get more involved."

✓ I have the right to be myself without changing to suit others.

✓ I have the right to change a relationship when my feelings change. I have the right to say, "We used to be close, but I want something else now."

✓ I have the right not to want physical closeness.

✓ I have the right to dress and act the way I want to without promising to have sex.

✓ I have the right to say no.

Source: "Acquaintance Rape: When the Rapist Is Someone You Know," Illinois Coalition Against Sexual Assault, 1996.

a woman sexually without her consent. Another surprise was that 84 percent of the men who had committed rape as it is legally defined said that they thought what they'd done wasn't rape.[4] In another survey of male college students, 51 percent said they might rape a woman if they knew they wouldn't get punished.[5]

The survey also found that college women were confused about the definition of rape. Only 27 percent of the women who had been raped thought that what had happened to them was rape.[6]

Mistaken attitudes about rape are formed at an even younger age. The Rhode Island Rape Crisis Center did a survey of 1700 sixth through ninth graders about their attitudes toward rape. They were asked whether or not a man has the right to force a woman to have sex if he spent money on her. Nearly 25 percent of the boys and 16 percent of the girls said yes. When asked whether or not it was okay to force sex if they'd dated for six months, 65 percent of the boys and 47 percent of the girls said yes.[7]

The truth, of course, is that the length of time a couple has been dating, the amount of money he's spent, or any other excuse a guy can dream up doesn't give him the right to have sex with a girl who doesn't want it.

The Role of Alcohol and Drugs

There are many statistics that show the connection between being drunk and either raping or being raped:

> A study published in a psychology journal showed that 26 percent of the men who admitted raping were drunk, and another 29 percent were "somewhat buzzed"—a

total of 55 percent had used alcohol. Of the women who were raped, 21 percent were drunk and 32 percent "buzzed"—a total of 53 percent.[8]

➢ In the *Ms.* magazine study, 75 percent of men and 55 percent of women involved in date rape said they had used alcohol or other drugs before it had happened.[9]

➢ A Duke University study showed that in 90 percent of all campus rapes, the rapist, the victim, or both had been drinking.[10]

➢ A 1995 University of Wisconsin, Madison, study showed 69 percent of those surveyed had been drinking before they were raped, and 74 percent of victims said the person who raped them had been drinking.[11]

Clearly, drinking to excess is a dangerous thing to do.

If you are a male, drinking too much can blur your thinking, make you more aggressive, and make it seem okay to do something you would never do if you were sober. A judge and jury won't care that you were drunk—you are responsible for what you do, including how much you drink and what you do as a result of that drinking. Rape is always the rapist's fault, no matter who was drinking or how much.

If you are a female, drinking too much may also blur your thinking and judgment, so you might miss the warning signals you would see if you were sober. If you are drunk, you may not be able to think clearly enough to resist or to see and act on a chance to get away. If you pass out, you can be raped and not even know it. Rape is never the

victim's fault even if she was drunk. In a perfect world a woman who is of legal drinking age should be able to drink as much as she wants and still be safe and have her "no" respected. But this is not a perfect world. Although getting drunk never makes rape the victim's fault, it can put a person in a very dangerous situation.

*A*lcohol is a strong factor in most cases of date rape. Seventy-five percent of men and 55 percent of women involved in date rape said that they had used alcohol or drugs before it happened.

As if alcohol weren't enough trouble, there's now something new—drugs that can make a victim pass out and be unaware of what is happening to her. The brand name of one of these drugs is Rohypnol® (generic name: flunitrazepam). It is a relative of tranquilizers like Valium but many times more powerful. Some of its street names are roofies, rope, the forget pill, and roach. Someone who is high on this drug is often said to be "roached."

The drug is illegal in this country, but it is prescribed in other countries, especially Mexico, to treat sleeping disorders. In small doses it causes a drunk feeling; in slightly larger doses it can knock the victim unconscious for up to twenty-four hours. When mixed with alcohol, it can be deadly. The drug put rock star Kurt Cobain into a coma for a time. Eventually, he would commit suicide.[12]

Rohypnol tablets are round and white, a little smaller than an aspirin. The drug has no taste or smell and dissolves quickly. Men have slipped it into women's drinks so that they would pass out and could easily be raped. Rohypnol manufacturer Hoffmann-LaRoche now coats the pills with a dye so that a drink it's dissolved in will turn blue, but not all manufacturers of flunitrazepam do that. The drug can cause memory blackout, so the woman may have no idea what happened. It can be found in urine for up to seventy-two hours, so if a woman suspects she might have been drugged and raped,

*T*he late Kurt Cobain (right) poses with fellow Nirvana band members at an MTV Video Music Awards show in 1993. Cobain once fell into a coma from using Rohypnol®.

Facts About Rohypnol

✓ The most common date rape drug.

✓ Illegal in this country; smuggled in.

✓ Same family as tranquilizers Valium and Xanax.

✓ Tablets in foil-backed blister packs.

✓ Colorless, odorless, and tasteless. May be ground into powder. Can be dissolved in a drink.

✓ Acts very fast—victim becomes sleepy within twenty minutes.

✓ Victim looks and acts drunk—slurred speech, difficulty in walking.

✓ Can cause loss of memory of what happens after it is taken.

✓ If combined with alcohol, can cause low blood pressure, difficulty in breathing, coma, death.

✓ Street names: roofies, ruffies, rophies, roches, roaches, la rochas (from the manufacturer's name Roche stamped on the tablets), rope, rib, forget pill, poor man's quaalude, R-2s, circles, dulcitas, whiteys, trip-and-fall, mind-erasers, Mexican Valium, lunch money (it's cheap), pappas, potatoes (from the mental capacity of someone who has taken it), negatives, minuses (from the markings on the one-milligram tablets), pluses or roches dos (from the markings on the two-milligram tablets).

Sources: "Rapists Are Using a New Weapon to Overpower Their Victims" brochure from Rape Treatment Center, Santa Monica-UCLA Medical Center, 1997, and author interview with Gail Safian, Hoffmann-LaRoche, Inc., August 7, 1998.

she should have a urine test right away. Rape crisis centers or police departments can get the testing done for free by a drug manufacturer.[13]

Another drug is GHB (for gamma hydroxy butyrate), sometimes called grievous bodily harm,

Facts About GHB

✓ Not as common as Rohypnol.

✓ Powerful central nervous system depressant.

✓ Acts very fast, within fifteen minutes.

✓ Causes dizziness, nausea, vomiting, confusion, seizures, intense drowsiness, unconsciousness, and coma.

✓ Can cause memory loss also.

✓ Life-threatening if combined with alcohol.

✓ Homemade in street labs, kitchens, or bathtubs, so strength is not the same between batches.

✓ Narrow margin between dose that causes intoxication and dose that causes coma and death.

✓ Clear liquid or white powder; colorless when dissolved, odorless, slightly salty taste.

✓ Street names: grievous bodily harm, liquid X, liquid E, liquid ecstasy, G, vita-G, G-juice, Georgia home boy, great hormones, somatomax, bedtime scoop, soap, gook, gamma 10, energy drink.

Sources: "Rapists Are Using a New Weapon to Overpower Their Victims" brochure from Rape Treatment Center, Santa Monica-UCLA Medical Center, 1997, and author interview with Gail Safian, Hoffmann-LaRoche, Inc., August 7, 1998.

liquid ecstasy, great hormones, liquid X, or other names. It is a clear liquid that can be made by amateurs in a bathtub. GHB is a terribly dangerous drug because it's a central nervous system depressant, which means it can shut down breathing. Sometimes it is sneaked into drinks, but other times it's just passed around in a water bottle or jar. It is colorless and odorless, but it has a somewhat salty taste, which is sometimes disguised by mixing the drug with a sweet-tasting liquor or soft drink.[14]

There are also a couple of other, less well-known drugs. One is burundanga, a drug that comes from Colombia and makes people forget what's happened to them. Another one is ketamine, a veterinary anesthetic used during surgery on animals. It's sometimes stolen from veterinarians' offices.[15]

Gail Safian, who works for a company that tests urine for the presence of drugs, says,

> Of 1,094 samples submitted to us for testing, only six had Rohypnol and forty-six had GHB. But about 40 percent had more than one drug. We see more alcohol, marijuana, and cocaine than the other drugs. We find that most often the drugs are taken voluntarily rather than slipped into a drink. The best protection is being aware of what you do.[16]

Some men have the idea that if a woman drinks or takes drugs to the point that she doesn't know what's going on, or if she has passed out, they can get away with having sex with her. But the federal law called the Drug-Induced Rape Prevention and Punishment Act of 1996 makes it a crime punishable by up to twenty years in prison for anyone to use a controlled substance to commit a violent crime, including sexual assault.[17]

The best advice for avoiding alcohol or drug-influenced rape: Don't drink while you are underage (both guys and girls). When you are of legal age, don't drink so much that you get drunk. Never take illegal drugs. Always keep your eyes on your drink, and don't drink anything that's being passed around in a group of people.

Chapter 4

Am I at Risk for This Awful Thing?

Heather, who was discussed earlier, was nice, friendly, and outgoing. She really wanted to have a boyfriend, so when Kevin came into her life, she was thrilled. He was her first love, and she thought she'd stay with him forever. That's why she had sex with him. Later, she found out it wasn't going to last forever.

Jenny, also discussed earlier, was very young and very innocent. She'd never been on a date and was just starting to notice boys.

Bobbi, another girl of high school age, had much more experience than either Heather or Jenny. She started dating when she was only twelve. She always had a lot of boys around and had had sexual relationships with many of them.

Which of those girls is at risk for date rape?

The truth is, they all are.

Risk Factors for Being Raped

Besides the statistics quoted before—showing that women between the ages of eighteen and twenty-nine are at the greatest risk[1], and the age seems to be moving down—there are some other factors that can put a girl at higher risk of being raped.

Not knowing your own limits. According to Janine Arseneau, both girls and guys need to think about their personal standards. "You need to know where you draw your own personal line—at what point you will say no—long before you go on a date," she says,

> Have a talk with yourself as a way of thinking it through: "Maybe someday, when I'm eighteen or twenty-one, or when I'm married, I will choose to have sex. Before that time, I'd like to go on dates. I wouldn't mind kissing. I wouldn't mind touching but only a certain kind." Most people don't think about those things in advance. They wait until there's a fire and then think about how to douse it.[2]

Not having a plan. Another risk factor, is not planning in advance what you would do if a date tried to pressure you into having sex. Again, the key to reducing risk is to think about it before it happens, before you are on a date, maybe before you've even met a guy you want to date. You need to plan not only when you will say no, but how you will say it. You have to think about what you would do if you were ever in a bad situation. "It's uncomfortable to think about," Arseneau warns, but not thinking about it can put you at higher risk. "If you wait until you are in a car with a guy to consider what you'd do if he wanted to have sex with you, it's far too late."[3] Think about what you would do in various situations: Talk about it with your parents, a teacher, your friends. Have a plan in mind.

Your plan might include the following:

➢ My first dates with a new guy will be group

things. I won't go out alone with him until I know him better.

➤ I won't go out with guys who are much older than I am.

➤ I won't go to an isolated place alone with a guy, or to his room if no one's home.

➤ I won't drink on a date as long as I'm underage. When I am of legal age, I won't drink so much that I don't know what's going on.

➤ I'll talk to my parents about having a cell phone with me when I'm on a date.

➤ I'll carry enough money with me to get home by cab or bus if I have to.

➤ I'll arrange a code word with my parents that they will know in a phone call means "come and get me right away."

These are just examples. Your own list may be quite different. And you'll probably be able to think of many more precautions.

Risk Factors for Committing Rape

It's not just girls who need to think ahead, though. Only men can stop rape. Guys, too, need to think about their own standards and how they will treat the girls they date. They need to evaluate their beliefs to see if they are at risk of becoming a date rapist. If you're a guy of dating age, ask yourself these questions:

When do I plan to have sex? Will you wait until you're at a certain age? Will you wait until you're married? Before that time, what do you think is okay and not okay to do sexually? Know your own personal standards and limits—and make them yours, not your friends'.

Do I think when the guys in the locker room are bragging about scoring that I have to join in? Do you think that if you don't have anything to report, you're somehow not a "real man"? Real men set their own standards and live up to them; they don't do what the other guys are doing just to be part of the group.

Do I believe that a girl ever owes me sex? Do you think a girl will owe you if you spend money on her or if you've been going out with her for a long time? Do you think she should give in to you if she's had sex before? Do you feel as if you own her if she's your girlfriend? If your answer is yes to any of these questions, you need to rethink your attitudes.

Do I think I should be in charge and make all the decisions just because I'm a guy? Especially sexual decisions? If that's your belief, then, again, you need to rethink it. A girl is your equal and has an equal say in any relationship.

Do I believe that when I'm turned on sexually I can't be expected to stop? If you do, you need to know that being turned on is no excuse for rape.

Do I think that if I've been drinking, I can't be held responsible for what I do? A judge or jury will definitely hold you responsible.

Do I think that if a girl can't say no because she's drunk or drugged, it's okay to have sex with her? If so, you need to learn real fast that having sex with anyone who is out of it is legally rape.[4]

Early Warning Signs

Many young women who are date raped see signs of trouble long before the actual assault. Unfortunately,

Communication Can Help

What women can do:

✓ Know your sexual desires and limits.

✓ State your desires and limits clearly.

✓ Be assertive.

✓ Be aware that your nonverbal actions may send messages that you don't intend.

✓ Pay attention to what is happening around you.

✓ Trust your intuition. If you feel afraid, get out of the situation.

✓ Be aware that nothing you do is a guarantee against sexual assault.

What men can do:

✓ Know your sexual desires and limits.

✓ State your desires and limits clearly.

✓ Accept the woman's limits. Listen to her and assume she means what she says.

✓ Do not assume that previous permission for sexual contact means that she wants to have sex again.

✓ Understand that being turned down for sex is not a rejection of who you are as a person. It means your partner does not want sex with you at that time.

Source: "Aquaintance Rape: When the Rapist Is Someone You Know," Illinois Coalition Against Sexual Assault, 1996.

too many of them ignore the warnings until it's too late. Why would anyone ignore warning signs? For a couple of reasons.

Probably the major reason for ignoring warning signs is not wanting to be rude or to be embarrassed if their suspicions aren't true. "I'll look silly if I'm wrong," she thinks. "He'll be mad if he really wasn't going to do anything, and he might not ask me out again." So she waits until it's too late to react successfully.

Another reason is that girls are too often brought up to be "nice," to smile and not make trouble. So when they realize they are in danger of being raped, they don't want to make a fuss. They may like the guy, they may know his family or friends, or they may be part of the same school group or work together. So they keep quiet and are raped.

What are some early warning signs that you might be in danger? Keep these in mind:

> Do you have a sense that something isn't right? Are you uncomfortable with him? Is there some vague uneasiness buried inside? If so, that's your instinct talking. Listen to it.

> Does he make you feel bad about your self? Does he put you down, tell you you're dumb, or make jokes at your expense?

> Does he put down women in general? Does he tell dirty jokes or make cracks about "dumb broads"?

> Does he use his body to control you— blocking your way, standing between you and the door, grabbing your wrists? Does he not respect your personal space, standing

too close or rubbing against you? Does
he do disrespectful things like snapping
your bra or grabbing your breasts?

➤ Does he try to run your life by telling you
what to wear, whom to be friends with, or
how to spend your time? Does he insist on
always making all the decisions about
which movie to see or whom to spend
time with?

➤ Is he jealous and possessive, accusing you
of flirting or cheating? Does he say you
belong to him?

➤ Is he verbally abusive? Studies show that
75 percent of verbal abusers turn to
physical violence within a year.[5] Batterers
and rapists often use verbal abuse as the
first step.

➤ Does he pressure you to use illegal drugs
or alcohol?

➤ Is he violent or rebellious? Does he have
brushes with the law, fool around with
weapons, or hang out with "scary" guys?

➤ Is there a history of abuse in his family?

➤ Does he mistreat you and then blame you
for it?

➤ Do your friends or family not like him?[6]

If you answer yes to even two of these questions,
you may be in danger from that particular guy. But
keep in mind that a guy who doesn't do any of those
things can also be capable of date rape.

Chapter 5

What to Do If It Is Happening

If either Heather or Jenny had seen what was coming, she might have been able to take some steps to protect herself. Only a rapist can stop a rape, but women can take some preventative measures. It is important to remember, however, that if prevention doesn't work and the rape happens anyway, it is never the victim's fault for not "trying" hard enough. Rape is always the rapist's fault.

A woman, however, can lower her risk of being a victim of date rape, both in advance and while the man is trying to rape her.

Lowering Your Risk Long Term

"The best thing you can do to lower your risk of becoming a victim of date rape," says Janine Arseneau, "is to develop your self-esteem."[1]

Can self-esteem—feeling good about yourself—prevent date rape? Yes. "Self-esteem means feeling comfortable with yourself, so when you say no you know you have that right and feel good about it," Arseneau says. "You don't have to second-guess yourself about whether you should have said yes to please the other person. You know you are an important person and don't have to give in to what someone else wants you to do."[2]

Other suggestions come from both Arseneau and the *Ms.* magazine survey:

> ➤ Know your own limits, but don't stop there. Communicate them. You have the right to tell your date your limits. Don't force a guy to guess what you want and don't want to do. He's not a mind reader.

> ➤ Be assertive. Don't think that being feminine means being passive and doing whatever a guy wants. Stand up for yourself.

*Y*oung women should get to know a guy before going out alone with him. Group activities or double-dates allow a girl to safely learn what a potential date is really like.

➤ Get to know a guy before you go out alone with him. Double-date first, and ask people who know him what he's like. Picking up strange guys is dangerous.

➤ Keep control. Don't put your date in complete charge. That might mean paying for part of the date yourself so that he won't feel you owe him anything. It might mean driving yourself sometimes. It might mean having a buddy or family member you can call for a ride at any time. It might mean carrying a cell phone if that's possible, or money for a pay phone or a cab. It might even mean taking a self-defense course.

➤ Listen to your feelings; trust your instinct. If you hear a little voice whispering, "Watch out, this guy might be bad news," listen to it. Bad vibes usually have some basis in fact. Being overly cautious is better than taking a chance and later wishing you had not.[3]

What if you've done all those things—you know the guy, he seems polite, you've told him how far you are willing to go sexually—but you're still in trouble? He's coming on too strong, touching you in ways you don't want, pushing you down—you know he's getting ready for sex, and you don't want it. What then?

Two university researchers asked more than two thousand women college students about their experience with rape or near rape. About two hundred of them said they had managed to avoid rape. The researchers interviewed them to find out how they did it. What they found was very interesting.

The first thing they discovered was that women who successfully avoided rape were the ones who felt the least guilty, who didn't blame themselves for the guy's attempt. In other words, they had high self-esteem and were able to think, "He doesn't have the right to do this to me. It's not my fault he's trying."

Second, they found the women who avoided rape were the ones who took some action. They screamed, they ran away, they didn't sit there and worry about the right thing to do. They just acted.

Arguing with the guy, reasoning with him, or crying were less effective than screaming and running.[4]

Some additional advice:

> Try to stay calm. It's hard, but you need to be able to think. Even if you decide to scream and run, you need to do so deliberately, knowing what you're doing, rather than in a panic.

> When you figure out what's going on, act

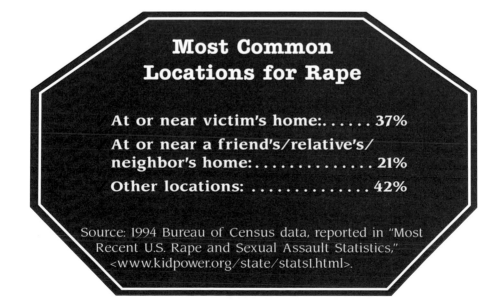

Most Common Locations for Rape

At or near victim's home:. 37%

At or near a friend's/relative's/ neighbor's home:. 21%

Other locations: 42%

Source: 1994 Bureau of Census data, reported in "Most Recent U.S. Rape and Sexual Assault Statistics," <www.kidpower.org/state/stats1.html>.

quickly. Look around and judge your situation. Are there people around who will hear you? How far are you from a safe place if you run? How violent is the guy? Once you decide what to do, go for it. He won't wait while you debate.

➤ Be rude. If he's out of line, you don't have to be polite and spare his feelings. Do and say whatever is necessary to get him to back off.

➤ Get away if you can. Get out of the car, run out of the house, and run to where there are people, even into a restaurant or store. Some women have been embarrassed to run because the guy had torn off part of their clothes. This is no time to be modest. Running away half dressed is better than being raped.

➤ Make noise. Scream, yell, or honk the car horn. Try to let people know where you are. Yelling, "Help—I'm in the science room" is better than just screaming, because rescuers won't have to guess where you are.

➤ If you can't run or scream, try talking. Don't try to argue with him, but rather get him involved in a conversation. Some women have told the guy they want to have sex but need to go to the bathroom first; then they ran. Or they've said they have a disease like AIDS or herpes, or that they have their period. Some have acted crazy, or done something disgusting like vomiting to take the "romance" out of it for him. These things don't always work, but if it's the only option, they're worth a try.

➤ There is no hard and fast rule about fighting back. But if you do decide to fight, be prepared to hurt him. A halfhearted struggle will usually only make him angry. You have a better chance of succeeding if you've taken a self-defense course. Never fight if he has a weapon. If he seems to be a sadistic rapist who takes joy in causing pain, fighting back can be dangerous. You'll have to decide what to do based on your individual situation, how confident and prepared you are, and knowing that resisting means taking a chance of making him angrier.[5]

All this advice may make it sound as if you can always prevent a date rape and that if you are raped, it's your fault for not trying harder. Nothing could be farther from the truth. Sometimes, no matter what a woman does to resist, the rape happens. It is never her fault, no matter how much or how little she resisted. It is always the rapist's fault.

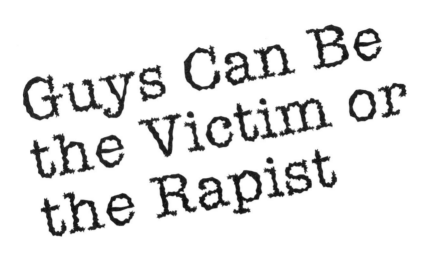

Chapter 6

Guys Can Be the Victim or the Rapist

The subject of men and sexual assault is complicated because men involved in rape can have two very different roles. On one hand, they are sometimes the victims of sexual assault. On the other hand, in most cases, they are the ones who do the raping.

When a Guy Is the Victim

The statistics about male rape may surprise you—it happens more often than many people think. Both adult men and young boys can be victims of rape. About one in six boys will be sexually assaulted by age eighteen.[1] The majority of these, almost 70 percent, will be raped by other men.[2]

"There are some adults who are sexually stimulated by children and adolescents," says Randy Neff, a social worker who works with teenagers. "Most of them are heterosexual, some are homosexual, some are bisexual."[3]

Neff points out that young men are rarely raped by strangers. Usually it is an acquaintance rape, often done by someone they trust. It may be a teacher, a coach, a family friend, or an older teen that the younger boy thinks is a friend. Sometimes the sexual activity is just touching; often the rapist wants the victim to touch him. Sometimes, though, it can include penetration of the anus or mouth.

Guys who are raped go through the same feelings that women do—fear, anger, humiliation, pain. In addition, a young man who is raped by another man may worry that the rape means he is a homosexual. He may think the rapist picked him because he sensed the victim was really

*G*uys who are raped can often experience the same anger, humiliation, and pain that women do.

gay. This is not true. "A homosexual rape definitely does not make a boy gay," Neff says.[4]

Also, while he may not have wanted the sexual activity, the victim's body may have responded. "Our bodies are wired so that sex is pleasurable," Neff says. "A boy's body may respond even though it's abuse and he is not gay. That response may make the victim feel unnecessarily guilty."[5]

There are some warning signs guys should be aware of, Neff says.

➢ Another man, especially an older one, being "too friendly." An adult may groom kids he wants to have sex with by being very warm and friendly. He may begin to bring sex into the friendship through jokes, sexual remarks, or showing the victim pornography. If you are ever uneasy about attention from another male, listen to your instinct. Ask another adult if you aren't sure if something is okay.

➤ A man telling you to keep something secret. If you shouldn't tell anyone about it, you probably shouldn't be doing it.

➤ A man offering you drugs or alcohol if you are underage.

If you are ever approached sexually by an adult, there are two very important things to do:

➤ Say no. Just like with girls and date rape, you've got to say no loudly and clearly. Even if the person has some authority in your life (like a teacher), he doesn't have the right to control you in this way.

➤ Tell someone—your parents, a teacher, a counselor, or some other adult. Even if the man backs off, he may try the same thing with someone else if he isn't stopped.[6]

Guys can also be the victim of a female rapist. It is possible to stimulate a male so that he has an erection even if he doesn't want to. It is also possible for a woman to threaten a man verbally ("Have sex with me or I will tell everyone you couldn't"). While it's rare, it does happen.

"It's especially confusing for a guy because the popular culture tells him that this is the most wonderful thing that could happen to him—a woman having sex with him," says Neff. "But it doesn't feel right, it's uncomfortable, creepy. Does that mean you don't like sex, that you're not normal, that you might be gay? No. It means someone took advantage of you."[7]

When a Male Is the Rapist

We can talk forever about ways for women to reduce their risk of date rape, but the fact is that date rape will only end when guys who are not victims themselves decide it will end. Men have the power to stop every kind of rape. But it will take a change in attitude for many of them.

According to Janine Arseneau, guys need to learn not to take it as personal defeat when girls say no. "If she says she's not ready to have sex, that doesn't mean you're a bad person," she says. "It simply means that for her, right now, it isn't a good thing. It's not a put-down of you, and it isn't an invitation to you to try harder."[8]

> If you push a girl into having sex, it won't be satisfying, consensual sex for either of you. It will just mean you were stronger or more powerful than she was, and you got her to give in. That's not winning, that's not conquering, that's not something that feels good. That's doing something awful to another person. There's a word for it. The word is rape.[9]

Instead, think about how you would feel if your mother or sister were raped. Would you see that as a score? As something to feel good about? Think about how you would feel if your family and friends found out you had committed a crime. "Would you like yourself then?" Arseneau asks. She goes on to say,

> Date rape is the same as holding someone up with a gun. It's taking something from someone else. The person you've done it to will never, ever be able to forget it. You've taken something from

her that she will never be able to get back. It's not about sex, it's about her dignity, her sense of herself as a person, her feeling that her body belongs to her, her sense of safety. That's a terrible thing to have to live with, both for you and for her.[10]

To prevent date rape from happening ever again to any woman, adopt these guidelines as your own:

➤ Don't ever force or even pressure a girl into having sex. It doesn't matter if you've had sex with her before, if she's had sex with your friends, if you've been going out a long time, if you've spent a lot of money on her, or if she's let you kiss and touch her sexually. She has every right to say no at any time and at any stage of a relationship, and you must respect that.

➤ Remember that drinking too much or taking drugs can make you more aggressive and blur your judgment to the point that you might do things you wouldn't otherwise do. Remember, being drunk or high is no excuse. Many guys who said, "But it wasn't my fault. I was drunk," have ended up in jail. Don't believe the myth that if a girl is drunk, she's

*G*uys should never try to pressure someone into having sex with them. Even nagging is a form of pressure and should not be done to a young woman.

asking to be raped. No one ever asks or deserves to be raped.

> ➤ Don't join other guys in a group sexual experience. If a girl is having sex with a group of guys, it most often isn't her choice, especially if she's had too much to drink. This behavior is called gang rape. Don't believe it when the other guys say she's really enjoying it. Instead, try to stop it or, if you can't, leave and call for help.

> ➤ Don't confuse sex with love or with being "a man." Sex can be a close emotional experience if it's by mutual consent. It's never a close experience for a girl who is pushed into it. You can have sex with every girl you date and still not experience love. Scoring "points" won't make you a better man.

> ➤ Ask a girl what she wants if you aren't sure. Don't assume. If her answer is no, stop. Don't pressure, don't argue, don't tell her that she "really wants it" while you overpower her. If she says she doesn't, then she doesn't. Continuing after she says no is rape.

> ➤ When your buddies brag about how many girls they've scored with, let them know they're acting like jerks. Stand up for what's right. You may take some flak at first, but in the long run you'll earn their respect—and certainly the respect of the girls who hear about it.[11]

Chapter 7

If It Happens to You

Neither Heather nor Jenny told anyone about what had happened to her until years later. That's not unusual. Far too many victims of date rape try to carry the burden alone. One study reported that only one in five date rape victims even tells her parents.[1]

A University of Pennsylvania study found five reasons why victims don't tell their families:

> ➢ To protect them from emotional pain.

> ➢ Out of fear that parents wouldn't under-stand because of their attitudes about rape or their disapproval of what the victim was doing (drinking, being alone with a date).

> ➢ They want to stay independent and are afraid their families will clamp down on them.

> ➢ They just don't feel close to their parents.

> ➢ They live on their own, too far away to want to involve their families.[2]

Some of these reasons may be valid for some young women. But for most victims of date rape, trying to cope alone just makes the trauma worse.

The Reality of Date Rape

Date rape victims experience a whole swirl of emotions—so many that they may not be able to sort out how they feel or what to do. The emotions may include fear, anger, pain, disbelief, or a desire for revenge. A victim may also feel guilty and blame herself for causing the rape because she believes she led him on—because she kissed him or dressed too sexy or was drinking. However, none of these things means the rape was the victim's fault. But feelings are not always logical.

A date rape victim may seem calm or composed, or she may be nearly hysterical. Later, she may find it hard to concentrate, or she may not be able to think of anything but the rape. She may have trouble sleeping or be jumpy, shaky, or have a rapid heart-beat. Many victims say they feel dirty and take shower after shower, trying to get clean again. Some victims become so fearful that they won't go out or be alone. They may not be able to trust even close friends and feel they aren't safe with anybody. They may see their rapist many times if they go to the same school or live in the same neighborhood: That can make their fear even worse. The victim's whole world may seem threatening, with no safe place to turn. Some victims talk easily about their fears and feelings, telling anyone who will listen. Others bury them deep.[3]

Long-term consequences can also be severe. Thirty-one percent of all rape victims develop post-traumatic stress disorder sometime in their lives.

Helping Someone Who Has Been Date Raped

▶

- ✓ Most important, believe her.
- ✓ Listen while she pours out her feelings—that will help her deal with them.
- ✓ Comfort her. Hold her if that's what she wants, give her a stuffed animal, make hot cocoa.
- ✓ Tell her that it wasn't her fault.
- ✓ Protect her. Let her stay with you if that's what she wants.
- ✓ Suggest that she call a rape crisis center.
- ✓ Help her gather evidence. Encourage her not to shower and to put each piece of clothing in a separate paper bag.
- ✓ Get medical attention. Even if she appears unhurt, she needs to see a doctor.
- ✓ Allow her to decide what to do. Offer suggestions, encourage, but don't decide for her.
- ✓ If you are her boyfriend, let her come back to physical affection when she's ready. Let her know you don't think she's "dirty," but don't force touch.
- ✓ Encourage her to get help, both through a counselor and a lawyer.
- ✓ Be there. Let her know she can talk to you even months later.
- ✓ Learn everything you can about date rape and what comes after.
- ✓ Get help yourself if you need it. Sometimes a friend, boyfriend, or family member needs to talk to a counselor, too.

Source: Robin Warshaw, *I Never Called It Rape: The* Ms. *Report on Recognizing, Fighting, and Surviving Date and Acquaintance Rape* (New York: Harper and Row, 1988), pp. 181-184.

Rape victims are also thirteen times more likely to attempt suicide than nonvictims.[4]

All these reactions are normal and apply equally to male victims.

Getting Help

"Most women who are date raped do heal and go on with their lives," says Janine Arseneau. "It doesn't go away, they don't forget what happened to them, but with time, this horrible act begins to recede into the background."[5]

But it's harder to heal if you try to do it alone. "For most women, it helps to talk to another person who has gone through it," she says.[6]

There is one major thing victims must understand so that they can heal, Arseneau says: "It wasn't your fault. You did nothing wrong."[7]

Some young women can tell their friends and families and get support from them. Others find they need to talk to a counselor. A rape crisis center is a good place to start. Many of the counselors there have been through a rape themselves. They know what you are feeling and how to help. Unfortunately, only 5 percent of victims use their services.[8]

Reporting the Rape

Many rape victims choose not to report the rape to the legal system. They may have reasons for that choice that are valid in their own minds (such as fear of the rapist or embarrassment), but they must realize that not reporting a rape allows the rapist to go free. Often he will repeat the rape with another victim. Amy Judy, the lawyer with the Wisconsin Coalition Against Sexual Assault, suggests that victims consider the following points before deciding whether or not to report:

➤ Successful prosecution teaches the rapist that what he did is a crime. It may stop him from doing it again.

➤ Reporting the rape helps let society know that date rape is a frequent, serious crime. It helps disprove the myths about rape that too many people believe.

➤ It helps victims regain a sense of control over their lives.[9]

"But in the end, it has to be up to the victim," Judy says. "We encourage victims to think about reporting, but we understand if they choose not to. Each person has to balance the pros and cons based on her own situation."[10]

Although procedures may vary a bit from state to state, in general, this is what you can expect to happen if you report a rape.

Why Most Rapes Aren't Reported

According to surveys, only 16 percent of all rapes are ever reported to the police. In a survey of victims who did not report, their reasons were

✓ Thought nothing could be done 43%

✓ Felt it was a private matter 27%

✓ Afraid of police response............. 12%

✓ Not important enough 12%

✓ Other 6%

Source: "Rape in America: A Report to the Nation," National Victim Center, April 23, 1992.

You will probably start by going to the police station or to a rape crisis center. Trained staff at such a center can help you report the rape to the authorities.

The police will launch an investigation. If the rape was recent, within seventy-two hours, the police will suggest you go to a hospital for a physical exam. There are doctors and nurses at the hospital who are trained in how to help rape victims. You will have to have an examination of your sexual organs (both outside and inside) for injuries, semen, hair, or skin cells from the rapist. The police may require you to leave the clothes you wore at the time of the rape, because clothing can hold important evidence.

After they have finished their investigation, the police will make a recommendation to the district attorney's office about whether or not to charge the rapist. The district attorney (D.A.) may want to do some additional investigating to find out if the case can be proved beyond a reasonable doubt. The D.A. may decide there isn't enough evidence to prove that it was rape, or he or she may decide there is enough evidence to charge the perpetrator. In that case, the D.A. will file a complaint with the criminal court. That begins the pretrial process.

The rapist may be arrested, or he may just get a summons telling him he has been charged with a crime and must appear before a judge at a certain time. At this first appearance, the charges will be read. The judge will look more closely at the evidence and decide if there is probable cause that a crime occurred. If there is, the defendant will enter a plea. If his plea is not guilty, a trial will be scheduled. Bail (a sum of money the suspect pays so that he or she can leave jail until the trial) may be set, and the accused then may be released.

The trial can be before either a judge or a jury; usually, it's the accused's choice. The verdict can go either way. Victims have to accept that sometimes a rapist will go free. But many victims will have the satisfaction of seeing the rapist punished.[11]

Seeking justice after a rape is a long procedure. The victim will have to testify and relive the rape, probably more than once. "It's a tough process. The level of reporting date rape is very low," Amy Judy says. "But there are people at rape crisis centers who understand the process and can help. We suggest victims use them."[12]

No one can make the decision to report or not for you. But whatever you decide, it is important to realize that you will heal, says Janine Arseneau. "This didn't happen just to you. There are thousands of women who have been sexually assaulted," she says.

> There are hundreds of thoughts that crowd into your head when you've been raped, and some-times they last for a very long time. The people who do best in terms of healing are those who are able to tell another person and get some sup-port, who realize it's just too big a secret to try to resolve on their own.[13]

If it happens to you, take advice from Heather and Jenny and from experts like Amy Judy and Janine Arseneau: Don't keep it a secret. Tell some-one and get help and support. Give yourself every chance to heal so that you can lead a normal life— a life that will include loving relationships in the future.

National Coalition Against Sexual Assault (NCASA)

125 N. Enola Drive
Enola, PA 17024
717-728-9764
FAX 717-728-9781
e-mail: ncasa@redrose.net
<www.achiever.com/freehmpg/ncas>

Rape, Abuse & Incest National Network (RAINN)

Toll-free, confidential rape crisis hot-line (can connect you to your local crisis center, twenty-four hours a day):
800-656-HOPE

Rohypnol information line:
Hoffmann-LaRoche
800-720-1076

Chapter 1: He Was My Friend—How Could He Do This?

1. Personal interview with anonymous, October 21, 1997.
2. Ibid.
3. Ibid.
4. Ibid.
5. Ibid.
6. Ibid.
7. Ibid.
8. Ibid.
9. Personal interview with anonymous, January 22, 1996, and October 23, 1997.
10. Ibid.
11. Ibid.
12. Ibid.
13. Ibid.
14. Ibid.
15. Ibid.
16. Ibid.
17. Ibid
18. Monte Williams, "Alex Kelly Receives a 16-Year Sentence in Girl's 1986 Rape," *The New York Times*, July 25, 1997, p. A1.

Chapter 2: It Isn't Always the Stranger Lurking in the Bushes

1. Personal interview with Janine Arseneau, July 17, 1997.
2. Personal interview with Amy Judy, September 23, 1997.
3. Judy interview.
4. Ibid.
5. "Rape in America: A Report to the Nation," National Victim Center, April 23, 1992, p. 4.
6. Ibid., p. 11.
7. "Acquaintance Rape: When the Rapist is Someone You Know," Illinois Coalition Against Sexual Assault, 1996, p. 1.
8. Adapted from author interviews with Amy Judy and Janine Arseneau and from Robin Warshaw, *I Never Called It Rape: The* Ms. *Report on Recognizing, Fighting, and Surviving Date and Acquaintance Rape* (New York: Harper and Row, 1988), pp. 18–20.
9. Warshaw, p. 98.
10. Ibid.

Chapter 3: Who Does This and Why?

1. Personal interview with Janine Arseneau, July 17, 1997.

2. "Acquaintance Rape: When the Rapist Is Someone You Know," Illinois Coalition on Sexual Assault, 1996, p. 4.

3. Linda Cassidy and Rose Marie Hurrell, "The Influence of Victim's Attire on Adolescents' Judgments of Date Rape," *Adolescence*, vol. 30, no. 118, Summer 1995, p. 322.

4. Robin Warshaw, *I Never Called It Rape: The* Ms. *Report on Recognizing, Fighting, and Surviving Date and Acquaintance Rape* (New York: Harper and Row, 1988), p.83.

5. Mary Koss and Mary Harvey, "The Rape Victim: Clinical and Community Interventions," Sage Library of Social Research, 1991, quoted in *Sexual Violence Facts and Statistics*, Illinois Coalition Against Sexual Assault, 1994, p. 3.

6. Warshaw, p. 26.

7. James Dobson, *Children at Risk* (Dallas, Tex.: Word Publishing, 1990), p. 258.

8. Charlene Muehlenhard and Melaney A. Linton, "Date Rape and Sexual Aggression in Dating Situations: Incidence and Risk Factors," *Journal of Counseling Psychology*, vol. 34, no. 2, April 1987, p. 192.

9. Warshaw, p. 44.

10. Duke University newspaper *The Chronicle*, June 9, 1994.

11. Laurel Crown and Linda Roberts, "Executive Summary of Sexual Violations Study," University of Wisconsin, Madison, 1995.

12. Jean Seligmann and Patricia King, "'Roofies': The Date-Rape Drug," *Newsweek*, February 26, 1996, p. 54.

13. "Rapists Are Using a New Weapon to Overpower Their Victims," Rape Treatment Center, Santa Monica, California, 1997.

14. Ibid.

15. Personal interview with Gail Safian, public relations department, Hoffmann-LaRoche, Inc., August 7, 1997.

16. Ibid.

17. Press release, National Coalition Against Sexual Assault, October 16, 1997.

Chapter 4: Am I at Risk for This Awful Thing?

1. "Rape in America: A Report to the Nation," National Victim Center, April 23, 1992, p. 13.

2. Personal interview with Janine Arseneau, July 17, 1997.

3. Ibid.

4. Ibid.

5. "Relationship Abuse: What Teens Should Know," Milwaukee Women's Center, brochure.

6. Ibid.

Chapter 5: What to Do If *It* Is Happening

1. Personal interview with Janine Arseneau, July 17, 1997.

2. Ibid.

3. Arseneau interview; Warshaw, pp. 153–157.

4. Joyce Levine-MacCombie and Mary P. Koss, "Acquaintance Rape: Effective Avoidance Strategies," *Psychology of Women Quarterly*, 1986, vol. 10, pp. 311–319.

5. Adapted from Susan Jacoby, "How to Spot and Resist the Rapist You Know," *Glamour*, February 1994, pp. 164–165, 200–201.

Chapter 6: Guys Can Be the Victim or the Rapist

1. Diane Russell, "The Incidence and Prevalence of Intra-familial and Extra-familial Sexual Abuse of Female Children," *Handbook on Sexual Abuse of Children*, Springer Publishing Company, 1988. Quoted in "Male Survivors of Sexual Assault Information Sheet," Wisconsin Coalition Against Sexual Assault, 1997.

2. Ibid.

3. Personal interview with Randy Neff, August 14, 1997.

4. Ibid.

5. Ibid.

6. Ibid.

7. Ibid.

8. Personal interview with Janine Arseneau, July 17, 1997.

9. Ibid.

10. Ibid.

11. Ibid.

Chapter 7: If It Happens to You

1. "Date Rape: The Scary Truth," *Teen*, April 1995, pp. 72–73.

2. 1979 study by A.W. Burgess and L.L. Holmstrom, reported in Warshaw, *I Never Called It Rape: The* Ms. *Report on Recognizing, Fighting, and Surviving Date and Acquaintance Rape* (New York: Harper and Row, 1988), pp. 125–126.

3. Adapted from Warshaw, pp. 68–71.

4. "Rape in America: A Report to the Nation," National Victim Center, April 23, 1992, p. 7.

5. Personal interview with Janine Arseneau, July 17, 1997.

6. Ibid.

7. Ibid.

8. Mary Koss and Mary Harvey, "The Rape Victim: Clinical and Community Interventions," Sage Library of Social Research, 1991, quoted in *Sexual Violence Facts and Statistics*, Illinois Coalition Against Sexual Assault, 1994, p. 3.

9. Personal interview with Amy Judy, September 23, 1997.

10. Ibid.

11. Ibid.

12. Ibid.

13. Arseneau, July 17, 1997.

Nonfiction

Bandon, Alexandra. *Date Rape*. New York: Crestwood House, 1994.

Benedict, Jeffrey. *Athletes and Acquaintance Rape*. Thousand Oaks, Calif.: Sage Publications, 1998.

Chaiet, Donna. *Staying Safe on Dates*. New York: Rosen Publishing Group, 1995.

Leone, Bruno, ed. *Rape on Campus*. San Diego: Greenhaven Press, 1995.

Levy, Barrie, ed. *Dating Violence: Young Women in Danger*. Seattle: Seal Press, 1991.

McShane, Claudette. *Warning: Dating May Be Hazardous to Your Health*. Racine, Wisc.: Mother Courage Press, 1988.

Miller, Maryann. *Drugs and Date Rape*. New York: Rosen Publishing Group, 1995.

Mufson, Susan, and Rachel Kranz. *Straight Talk About Date Rape*. New York: Facts on File, 1993.

Parrot, Andrea. *Acquaintance Rape and Sexual Assault: A Prevention Manual*. Holmes Beach, Fla.: Learning Publications, 1991.

———. *Coping with Date Rape and Acquaintance Rape*. New York: Rosen Publishing Group, 1993.

———, and Laurie Bechnofer, eds. *Acquaintance Rape: The Hidden Crime*. New York: John Wiley and Sons, 1991.

Shuker-Haines, Frances. *Everything You Need to Know about Date Rape*. New York: Rosen Publishing Group, 1990.

Warshaw, Robin. *I Never Called It Rape: The Ms. Report on Recognizing, Fighting, and Surviving Date and Acquaintance Rape*. New York: HarperPerennial, 1994.

Video

Fight Back: An MTV News Special Report. MTV Networks/MTV Music Television, and the Rape, Abuse & Incest National Network (RAINN). Available for free rental at Blockbuster Video stores.

Index